Lonely

Even When You're Not Alone

George Hatcher

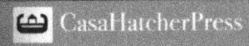 CasaHatcherPress

Printed in the United States of America and abroad.

This book can be purchased at over 44,000 bookstores and libraries, including brick-and-mortar stores and digital retailers such as Apple Books and Kindle.

Publisher:

Casa Hatcher Press, a Pretty Face, Inc. company

Rancho Mirage, California

Book Title: Lonely: Even When You're Not Alone

by George Hatcher

eBook ISBN: 979-8-9996764-5-0

Paperback ISBN: 979-8-9996764-4-3

LCCN: Pending

Introduction

Let's get something straight from the beginning:

I'm not a doctor.

I'm not a therapist.

I don't have a degree in psychology.

And I'm not a guru.

I'm just a guy who's lived a lot of life, made a lot of mistakes, and felt loneliness in ways most people don't talk about.

Everything in this book comes from personal experience — not from textbooks or lectures or certifications. And yeah, I've done some research. I've read the studies. I've tried to understand the science behind what loneliness *does* to a person. But at the end of the day, what you'll find in these pages isn't advice from an expert. It's a reflection from a survivor.

Introduction

I've been writing for over a decade. I've published more than 26 books. Not ghostwritten. Not farmed out. I sit with the keyboard and bleed the stories out myself. I only bring in help when it's time to edit.

Now, I don't have much formal education. I left school after the 9th grade. I did eventually earn my high school diploma while serving time in prison. And I'll be honest — I had to hustle for it. Back then, we didn't have money behind bars, but cigarettes were currency. I traded two cartons just to get a spot in the test queue. Do I think I *deserved* that diploma? I'm not sure. But I worked for it. I tell you this not to impress anyone — just to tell the truth.

That's what this book is: the truth. My truth.

It's about loneliness — what it feels like, what it steals from you, and how it sticks around long after the noise of life fades.

You won't find medical advice in these pages. You'll find stories. And if you see yourself in them, then maybe, just maybe, they'll help you feel a little less alone.

Because that's all I'm really trying to do.

Dedication

For Molly,

Many things have changed in the time it took to write these pages, but one truth remains as it has for over sixty years: you are the heart of every story I tell. Thank you for being my constant North, my quiet strength, and my greatest blessing.

All my love, always,

George

Also By George Hatcher

Mario Series:

Mario 1: Woman in Jeopardy

Mario 2: Coming of Age

Mario 3: Risky Business

Mario 4: Free Fall

Mario 5: Afire

Mario 6: Marked

Mario 7: Aftershock

Mario 8: Captivated

Single Titles:

One Wilshire

Gabi

Rico

Cats: Meow Is the Language of Love

HER: Artistic Expressions Through AI

Elegance in White: Through Wedding Gowns

Quinceañera Fashion: Fifteen & Fabulous

Billion Dollar Rainmaker Series:

Billion Dollar Rainmaker Part I

Pages of Passion Series:

Pages of Passion Book 1: My First 19 Years

Pages of Passion Book 2: Bold Beginnings

Pages of Passion Book 3: Rising Waves

Pages of Passion Book 4: Threads of Destiny

Non-Fiction / Other Works:

Beyond the Scale: Health Benefits of Keto for Wellness

Cool Under Pressure: Warm with Humor

Love Is What It Is: Lessons from Everyday Life

Living Fully While We Wait to Die: Mindfulness Amid Mortality

Ignite Your Potential: Break Free from the Ordinary

AfterLight: A Voice Beyond the Grave

Unfindable

Coming Soon

Chapter 1
Defining Loneliness

My wife and I have been married for sixty years. That's a long road — one filled with love, laughter, and, sure, more than a few bumps along the way. At one point, we both agreed it was best I move out. So, I did.

I packed up and left with my two cats. I rented an apartment, bought furniture for every room, and within two days, I was completely settled. I thought I had found freedom. I even bought a domain name: *magicofbeingalone*. I figured I was going to master solitude like some kind of art form.

But it didn't take long before the shine wore off.

Being alone — really alone — hit me harder than I expected. The quiet wasn't peace. It was hollow. I grew even closer to my cats during that time. I played with them more. Bought them toys. It wasn't just about keeping them entertained — it was about needing something, anything, to fill the space.

All that freedom to come and go without checking in with anyone? It became meaningless.

Just like that, I was back home in under three months.

* * *

I think I was about 18 — maybe just shy of 19 — when I landed in the military brig for going AWOL. I had split to Mexico right after marrying a beautiful woman from Juarez. That marriage didn't end well. Turns out, she was still seeing her ex-fiancé. I returned to the States and was sentenced to four months in a Marine brig.

Let me tell you — being locked up in the brig isn't like being bored in your room. It's chaos, 24/7. No time to sit around and feel sorry for yourself. You're too busy trying to survive. You're alert every minute, watching your back. Loneliness doesn't creep in there — not because you're not alone, but because survival drowns out everything else.

When I got out, two detectives from L.A. were waiting for me. A loan I never paid back — technically from my girlfriend's mother — got me charged with grand theft. That landed me in the Youth Authority. I served just under two years.

Now here's the thing: even though I had no problems with the other guys and felt reasonably safe, I was lonely in a way that stuck with me for decades. To this day, I can still feel that ache.

I couldn't even tell you exactly what I was lonely for. I had girlfriends in school. I had girls outside of school. But my heart was still tangled up with that woman from Juarez. I think I really loved her — or at least I believed I did when I said, "I do." She didn't even want to get married. I pushed it.

It wasn't one of those "she's pregnant" deals. Nothing like that. I was just young. And dumb.

Loneliness in jail? It's guaranteed. Doesn't matter if you're 18 or 80. You're going to feel it. Some folks say you get used to it after a few years. I'm not so sure. I have a friend who did 26 years inside. He's out now, and I never had the guts to ask if he was lonely. But I know he had to be. You can't do that kind of time and not carry that weight.

* * *

So what is loneliness to me?

After I got out of the Youth Authority, I hustled. Found a job, then another. Eventually, I went into business. I got married again — this time to a woman I'd been seeing for about a year. She became wife number two. That marriage lasted 24 days. Yeah, we made it a year dating, but 24 days after the wedding, it was over. Don't ask.

Then came wife number three. We had two kids together. But that relationship? We could count the number of days we actually lived together. I was a lousy companion — not mean, just absent. I worked constantly and ran my own businesses. She worked, too, independently. I barely noticed how lonely she must have felt, because I was too busy dealing with my own loneliness.

And how did I deal with it? I saw other women. It was just a thing. A distraction. I told myself it was because I was young. Immature. Blamed the age. But at some point, you're not 18 anymore. You can't keep telling yourself the same lies.

Then I married wife number four. And here we are, sixty years later — still together. You'd think that part of the story would be smoother, but nope.

Shortly after we married, I had to serve a year in the county jail for writing bad checks. Most of those checks were written before I even met her, tied to a business I was running.

Now, the facility wasn't awful. No bars. It was a sheriff's substation. I worked all day — washing cars, typing letters for the captain, running copies in the personnel department. They kept me busy. That helped. But the nights? That's when it got bad.

She'd come visit. Contact visits, thankfully. I could kiss her, put my arm around her, sit beside her for a while. But when those visits ended, and she walked out — that loneliness crashed in like a wave. Over and over again.

The loneliness was so obvious, even my letters gave it away. The officer who eventually drove me to the county jail to be released said, "George, we had bets at the station that you'd try to run. I read your letters — we thought we'd lose you." I guess my loneliness was leaking through every word.

Again, I wasn't free. Couldn't even make a phone call unless it was an emergency. It was a wreck. A train wreck.

And you know what? It doesn't matter that I caused it. People love to say, "Well, you did it to yourself." But that doesn't make it any easier. Loneliness doesn't care whose fault it is. It just shows up and sits with you, heavy and cold.

In those moments, I'd think about my wife. The woman I really loved. And even with all the mistakes, we're still here —

together. Doesn't mean the loneliness didn't tear through me. Because it did. And it still can.

Lonely is a bitch.

Chapter 2

Rebuilding the Self After Loneliness

Learning to Trust Life Again

Some people think the hardest part of being alone is the silence.

It's not. It's the way silence **makes you face yourself**.

When you've spent months — or years — in survival mode, loneliness doesn't always hit you right away.

Sometimes you're too busy fighting to notice what you've lost.

But eventually, when the chaos settles, and there's nothing left to fight...

you look around and ask:

What's left of me?

That's where the real rebuilding begins.

Not rebuilding your career, or reputation, or even your relationships.

Lonely

I'm talking about rebuilding *you*.

The self that got buried under all the mistakes, fear, and isolation.

The self that stopped trusting people.

Stopped trusting love.

Stopped trusting **life**.

* * *

I remember thinking at one point that I might never be the same again.

The brig shook something loose in me — like everything I believed about control and consequences and identity was scrambled.

And what came out of that experience was **not strength**, not right away.

What came out first was **emptiness**.

And then slowly, one hard truth at a time, I started putting myself back together.

* * *

You don't go back to being the person you were.

You become someone else — someone *wiser*, and if you're lucky, **more open**.

Rebuilding meant learning how to live without expecting the world to break me.

It meant forgiving myself for what I did when I was afraid.

It meant reaching for the phone instead of a bottle.

It meant writing instead of exploding.

It meant letting love find me again — *slowly*, on my terms, when I was ready to trust it.

There was a long stretch of time when I didn't feel *entitled* to connection.

I thought I had forfeited the right to be close to anyone.

But I came to understand something critical:

Loneliness doesn't mean you're broken. It means you're being invited to rebuild.

* * *

Tools for Rebuilding

• **Writing** was one of my lifelines.

It started in the brig, scribbled in the margins of a Bible. It continued when I got out, even when I didn't know what the hell I was writing about.

Writing gave shape to what I was feeling before I could speak it.

• **Routine** helped anchor me.

Waking up, making coffee, going outside. Something about the normalcy of it made the world feel stable again.

• **A few good people** made all the difference.

You don't need a crowd. Just a handful of people who treat you like you still matter — even when you don't feel like you do.

- **Faith, but not in the religious sense.**

Faith that *life wasn't done with me yet.* That I could still grow into something whole.

Rebuilding after loneliness is not a straight line.

Sometimes you relapse.

Sometimes you get close to people, and it scares you.

Sometimes the old voices come back, and you wonder if you were ever really worth saving.

But then you sit down, and you write, or you walk, or you call someone — and you keep showing up.

That's the work.

And eventually, little by little, you realize you've built a life you can live inside of again.

Chapter 3
Locked Up, Let Loose

What Came After the Brig

On the day of my release from the brig, I got what I thought I wanted.

Freedom.

But waiting for me, standing just past the gate, were two Los Angeles detectives.

Freedom didn't even last five minutes.

They read me my rights and handed me a copy of a warrant for grand theft.

I didn't even need to look at it. I already knew who it was.

Thelma.

Three charges. One thousand, one thousand, fifteen hundred. The loan that I didn't repay to my girlfriend's mom, who owed the $3500 to her friends that she borrowed the money from, so that she could lend it to me when I was sixteen years old.

Lonely

The forged letters from my real dad that he would repay the money on my behalf that I had shown to Thelma when she raised the money for me.

I didn't resist it.

I no longer fought anything.

The brig had worn me down.

County

Back behind bars — this time in Los Angeles County Jail — I was just **tired**.

Not scared, not tough. Just... worn down.

Six men, two bunks. That meant four of us on the floor. No room for privacy.

No room to think, unless you wanted to think about the smell, the fights, the clanking toilet inches from your face.

The brig had been worse — but this wasn't redemption.

This was **limbo**.

I met Mike there. All he did was fight and work out. If he wasn't punching someone, he was talking about punching someone.

I watched.

Listened.

And waited for my time to come.

* * *

The Deal

When my public defender showed up, he looked like something out of a courtroom cartoon: slick hair, cheap suit, smacking gum like he was chewing his way through the conversation.

"This is a sophisticated crime," he said. "Did you do this alone?"

"I did it," I said. "No need to dance around it."

He wanted to go to trial. Bring my dad in. Try to win it on a technicality.

I just wanted to be done.

Not to win — to be **done**.

"I want to get this over with," I told him.

The judge agreed to a plea. One count of grand theft.

And a sentence:

The California Youth Authority. Not to exceed three years.

He gave me credit for time served — four months in the brig, four in County.

Eight months in already. Eighteen years old.

And still not done.

Lonely

DVI

They sent me to DVI — Deuel Vocational Institute — in Tracy, California.

A Youth Authority prison. But don't let the name fool you.

DVI was no "youth" camp. It was hard time in a hard place.

They called it gladiator school — and they weren't joking.

Adults, gang members, lifers, predators — they were all in there.

And now, so was I.

But I was so beaten down by then... I didn't even care.

I walked into the yard like a man with no fight left.

And that's when I saw him.

Pi.

* * *

Homecoming in Hell

Pi had been my guy since Hollenbeck Junior High.

A force. A protector. A friend who never forgot you — no matter where you ended up.

"Ese," he said. "What the hell did you do?"

I laughed. "I'm guilty as sin."

He hugged me like a brother.

Suddenly, I wasn't alone anymore.

The guys around him — stone-faced and dangerous — nodded at me. Thumbs up. I was under Pi's wing now.

That meant something.

* * *

The Turn

I started classes.

Refrigeration. Air Conditioning. Typing. Accounting.

I'd failed at Hollenbeck — but here? I crushed it.

When survival isn't your full-time job, your brain starts to wake up again.

I wrote letters — a lot of them.

To Luna. To my parents. To myself.

Luna wrote back:

"I wish you had met me first and married me like you married my sister."

That line hit hard. So did the silence that followed after her last letter.

I didn't hear from her again.

But I kept writing.

* * *

The Yard

Lonely

Fights were constant. Blood was normal.

If you weren't in a gang, you were prey.

Mike — the guy from County — showed up one day, about to get jumped.

Ten guys closing in.

He didn't have a crew. No backup.

So I walked over.

Spoke up.

Dropped Pi's name.

That was enough.

Mike walked away.

We became tight after that. He joined my class.

And the guy who only knew how to fight?

Started learning to **build**.

* * *

Leaving

Eventually, the parole board cut me loose.

I'd done **twenty-one months** since coming back from Mexico.

The Navy Brig.

County Jail.

DVI.

When I walked out of those gates, I didn't cry.

I felt the burn in my eyes, the tightness in my throat.

But I held it back.

Until I hit the street.

Then I cried.

Quietly. For everything I'd done. For everyone I'd lost. For the man I still didn't quite know how to be.

* * *

📌 **And that's what loneliness is, too.**

It isn't always the cold silence in a cell.

Sometimes it's the slow realization that **you're the only one left to answer to.**

That's where I was.

Not just free.

But finally facing myself.

Chapter 4

When the Noise
Dies Down

You'd think freedom would feel louder.

After twenty-one months behind bars, I expected something like a roar — sirens, wind, voices, the street beneath my feet yelling "you made it."

But it wasn't like that.

It was quiet.

That quiet doesn't feel peaceful when you've been locked up.

It feels like a void.

Like you've finally escaped the noise, only to realize **you'd gotten used to it**. The banging. The shouting. The routine.

Now the silence felt like space... and space felt like loneliness again.

It wasn't about being alone.

It was about *not knowing where to land*.

* * *

What Comes After

I didn't walk out into a celebration. There was no family waiting at the gates.

No friend with a car, no job, no plan.

Just the same me — minus the rank, the uniform, the future I once thought I'd earn.

But I had my Bible.

The one I used to write in during the brig.

The one I got written up for, thrown into solitary for.

That small book was the only thing I walked out with that actually held **part of me**.

That Bible had more of my story in it than anyone on the outside did.

I went home to my parents for a while.

Tried to stay invisible. Tried not to be a burden.

They were kind in that quiet way parents are when they're too tired to say much, but still hold out some hope for you.

They gave me space.

Still, nothing about being out was easy.

You can get used to a cage if you live in it long enough.

You know the rules. You know the routine. You know who you are.

But out here?

I didn't know anything anymore.

* * *

Writing (Again)

It took me time, but I found myself sitting at the kitchen table one night.

No noise. No shouting. Just me, a pen, and a page.

And I wrote.

Not letters. Not Bible margins. Just **thoughts**.

Memories. Pain. Stuff I couldn't say to anyone else.

I don't remember what I wrote exactly, but I know I felt lighter after.

That's when it hit me:

Writing was *still* the way out.

Not just a way to escape the brig, or pass time in DVI.

It was the way I could dig out from everything I'd buried inside.

That night, I wrote until my hand cramped.

Didn't even realize I'd started writing a life.

* * *

No Dramatic Ending

I didn't suddenly turn into a clean-cut guy with a job and a second chance and a dream.

Nah.

I stumbled through it. Fell back into trouble here and there. Made more mistakes.

Had more marriages. Broke things I wish I hadn't.

Got broken a few times too.

But something was different after that stretch of time.

I started to **look** at things.

Feel things.

Notice who was hurting, who was lying to themselves, who was putting on a face while dying on the inside.

I'd been that guy.

Hell, I still was — some days.

But little by little, I started to see loneliness for what it really is.

So Let's Talk About It

We act like loneliness is this thing that shows up when you're old.

When the house gets quiet. When your kids are gone. When your partner dies.

But the truth?

Lonely

Loneliness comes way before that.

It comes when you're seventeen and locked in a cell.

When you're nineteen, walking out of prison, free but lost.

It comes in a crowded room. In a marriage. In a phone call that doesn't come.

It comes when the lights go out and your thoughts get loud.

Loneliness is the space between **who you are** and **who you wish someone could see**.

And for me, that space has been wide for a long time.

But I'm still writing.

Still reaching.

Still trying to close that distance — for myself, and maybe for someone else reading this.

Chapter 5
Loving the Wrong Ghosts

Then there was Thelma.

Not a lover — not even someone close in that way.

She was the **mother of a girl I cared about**.

A girl I'd been close to — school friends, bed friends, tight but honest about not wanting to be more than that. We had no illusions, but maybe Thelma did. Maybe she thought one day her daughter and I would get married, settle down, make something real out of something young.

I don't know.

What I do know is this: when my brother got locked up in Mexico and my mom was falling apart because we didn't have the money to help him, **I panicked**. I was just a kid working at a drugstore after school. I wanted to fix it.

So I went to Thelma.

She made it easy — maybe too easy — to borrow the money.

$3,500 she didn't even have, so she borrowed it from her friends. And I lied to my mom and said I got the money from someone at the drugstore.

But then I ran.

Took off.

Got married.

Went to Mexico.

And Thelma? She had every right to be furious.

She probably went to the police, thinking they'd scare me into paying her back so she could repay her friends. But the police don't run a collection agency.

They filed **grand theft charges**.

I don't blame her for that.

It wasn't about revenge.

It was about desperation.

She wanted her life back — the one I accidentally burned a hole in.

There's **no question** I owed her the money.

There's **no question** I was wrong.

But it wasn't some big criminal scheme. It was a sixteen-year old **kid** trying to solve a grown-up problem, and doing it all wrong.

Chapter 6
The Shape Loneliness Takes

There's a part of loneliness people don't talk about — the **shapes** it takes.

Most folks imagine it as a shadow in the corner, a cold bed, a quiet room.

But it's more than that.

Loneliness isn't always still.

Sometimes, it's **loud**.

Sometimes it **moves**.

* * *

It Shows Up in the Mirror

After DVI, after the courtrooms and the concrete, I came home different.

Older? Maybe.

Wiser? Not really.

Just... altered.

I'd walk past a mirror and not recognize the guy looking back.

That's what happens when you've spent so long being watched — by guards, by other inmates, by people judging you.

When no one sees you for *who you are*, you stop seeing it yourself.

That's a kind of loneliness too — not knowing your own face anymore.

* * *

It Shows Up in Crowds

You'd think walking free would cure it.

But I could be in a crowded room, surrounded by voices and laughter, and still feel like I was underwater.

Because the truth is: **freedom doesn't fix isolation**.

I could breathe, yeah.

I could walk around.

But that *feeling* — that no one really knows you, or worse, **wants** to — it sticks.

Especially when you carry history like mine.

It's like having ink stains on your skin that only you can see.

You wonder if anyone would still hug you if they could read the whole story.

* * *

It Shows Up in Moments That Should Be Beautiful

There were nights I'd be sitting outside, air cool, stars out, maybe even with someone beside me — and I'd feel it.

This ache.

Like a hollow in my chest.

You ever feel that?

That *ache* when everything is fine, and you should feel happy... but something's missing?

That's loneliness, too.

It doesn't wait for tragedy.

Sometimes it creeps in when life is finally calm — because it knows that's when your guard is down.

* * *

And It Can Show Up After Growth

Even after all the time I did, after all the work to stay out of trouble, after the letters and books and changes —

I still felt it.

Because loneliness isn't just about other people.

It's about the **distance between who you've been and who you're trying to become**.

There's grief in that.

Even as you grow.

You miss the old you sometimes — even if he was broken.

Because at least you knew how he survived.

The new version?

You're still building him.

And sometimes, that's lonely work.

* * *

So What Do You Do With It?

You carry it.

But not like a wound.

Like a **compass**.

Because the truth is, if you can name your loneliness — if you can **face it** instead of stuffing it down — it can tell you where to go next.

Mine did.

It told me to write.

It told me to tell this story.

And it told me that maybe — just maybe — there's someone out there reading this who doesn't feel seen either.

Not really.

* * *

So if that's you?

Hey.

You're not broken.

You're not weird.

You're not "too much" or "too quiet" or "too hard to love."

You're just **human**.

And you're not alone anymore.

Chapter 7
The First Laugh After

There's a laugh you remember — the first one after the dark.

It's not loud.

It's not long.

But it feels **wrong**, almost. Like you're not allowed to feel that light again.

Like you're cheating grief. Or shame. Or survival.

But it comes out anyway.

And when it does...

You realize you're still alive.

* * *

I Think It Was Over Something Stupid

I don't even remember what the joke was.

Might've been a look someone gave me.

Might've been a movie.

Might've been a girl saying something that caught me off guard.

All I know is — it wasn't planned. It wasn't forced.

It just... came out.

That little laugh.

Like a cough with a smile in it.

And then the silence after, where I caught myself thinking,

"Wait... what the hell was that?"

It Felt Foreign

Because when you've been through what I've been through —

When you've been locked up, broken down, watched, punished, left behind —

You start to forget joy.

You get good at numb.

You get good at distracted.

You get good at just surviving.

But joy? That's a different language.

And I hadn't spoken it in a while.

Lonely

* * *

But That's How Healing Works

Not in big, dramatic moments.

Not in speeches. Not in therapy breakthroughs or giant realizations.

Healing shows up in a laugh you weren't expecting.

It shows up in a day where you don't think about the past for five whole minutes.

In a night where the silence doesn't feel like a punishment.

In a letter you write that isn't sad.

In the first time you feel *okay* being by yourself.

Tiny wins.

That's what healing is.

* * *

I Started Chasing That Feeling

Not the fake laughs. Not the bar scenes or the high-stakes hookups that left me emptier than I started.

No — I wanted that **honest**, stupid, accidental laugh.

The kind you get when you forget to be guarded.

The kind that surprises even you.

So I chased it in little ways.

Started walking just to walk.

Started reading again — not prison stuff, not escape stuff, just *stuff that made me curious*.

Started talking to people like they weren't threats or judges or therapists — just **people**.

I started seeing **light** again.

Not blinding, not overwhelming.

But enough to notice the color come back.

That Laugh Was a Marker

It didn't mean I was fixed.

It didn't mean I'd forgiven myself.

It didn't mean the loneliness was gone.

It just meant — **life wasn't done with me yet**.

And maybe, if you're reading this, you've had one of those moments too.

Or maybe it's still coming.

But it *will* come.

Because the dark never wins forever.

Lonely

And the fact that you're still here?

That's your proof.

Chapter 8

The Turning Point
– 42 Months That
Changed Everything

People ask me when things changed.

When I finally got tired of the cycle — bad checks, bad choices, always thinking I could outwork the consequences. I used to say, "This is the last time," more times than I can count. And I believed it every time. Until the last time became real.

Forty-two months.

That's what did it.

State and federal time. An eight-year sentence that got reduced.

But even reduced, 42 months is a long time to sit with yourself.

Before that, I'd been doing jail time in chunks. A few months here, a year there. In and out. Work-release programs, sheriff substations, county time. And in between? I'd run businesses, drink after five, try to hold on to a family life that was always cracked at the edges.

But this time?

This wasn't just a bump.

It was the wall.

The charge was grand theft.

I had bounced enough checks that they stopped calling it a mistake and started calling it a scheme. A pattern. A conspiracy.

The feds don't mess around when they decide you're a problem.

The only reason I wasn't buried under years was because I had enough sense to make restitution before sentencing. I'd built a strip center, paid off what I owed, and stood before a judge who — for reasons I still don't understand — gave me a break.

But the sentence still came.

And it came with clarity.

Those 42 months straightened me out.

I came home 39 years ago and haven't had a problem since.

That's not pride talking. That's just the truth.

Something inside me shifted during that time — maybe for the first time in my life. I stopped justifying my behavior. I stopped blaming the past. I stopped pretending I was the exception.

And I want to say this clearly, because people get it twisted:

The problem wasn't the money. It was the loneliness.

The loneliness that made me think I needed to be someone bigger, flashier, more powerful than I was.

The loneliness that made me believe a check could fill a hole.

The loneliness that made me chase escape in the form of status, alcohol, women, anything but truth.

I wasn't a drug user.

But alcohol? That was my escape hatch.

Not during the day. I didn't stumble around drunk. But every night, like clockwork, I'd hit that bottle. And every night, I'd tell myself it was just to unwind.

But really? It was to numb the guilt. The pressure. The disconnection.

And like any drug, it always asks for more.

So what changed?

Time.

Stillness.

Consequence.

And — more than anything — awareness.

I became aware of the wreckage behind me.

The marriages, the broken trust, the birthdays missed, the sons and daughters growing up without enough of me around.

Lonely

And I became aware of the life I still had a chance to live — if I didn't blow it.

Those 42 months were brutal.

But they were also a gift.

Because I finally heard what loneliness had been trying to tell me all along:

You can't fill a broken soul with distractions.

You have to stop.

Sit in it.

And rebuild — not your reputation.

Yourself.

And I did.

It took time.

It took work.

But I did it.

I haven't looked back.

That time in the system didn't just end when the gates opened. It followed me. In ways I didn't even understand yet.

Chapter 9

Lonely Doesn't Always Mean Alone

One of the hardest things to explain to people who haven't felt it is this:

You can be surrounded by people and still feel completely alone.

It's not about silence.

It's not about isolation.

It's about *disconnection*.

You can laugh at a joke, hold someone's hand, be in a room full of friends — and still feel like there's a wall of glass between you and the rest of the world.

* * *

I've Felt It in Beds, at Dinners, at Parties

There were nights I laid next to someone, their breath steady beside mine, and still felt like I was falling through space.

Lonely

I'd be at a gathering — music playing, drinks flowing, stories flying — and I'd smile, nod, maybe even joke around...

But part of me was floating above it all, watching, not *in* it.

Like I was playing a version of me that knew how to be social, how to belong —

But **underneath**, I was still that kid in the brig with a pencil and a Bible.

* * *

People Assume If You're Loved, You Can't Be Lonely

But that's not how it works.

Sometimes the loneliest you ever feel is when you *are* loved — but you know deep down they don't really **see you**.

Or maybe they *used to*, but not anymore.

Or maybe you've changed, and they're still clinging to the ghost of who you were before it all went sideways.

That disconnect?

That's loneliness in its sharpest form.

* * *

I Think That's Why Some People Sabotage Good Things

Because staying in something where you feel unseen hurts worse than walking away.

That's where I found myself more than once —

Walking away from good people, not because they did anything wrong, but because I couldn't feel real in front of them.

And if you can't be real, what's the point?

So you leave.

And the loneliness deepens — but at least now it feels honest.

* * *

But Here's the Flip Side

You can also be *completely alone* and not feel lonely at all.

When I started getting right with myself —

When I stopped trying to fix the past or prove anything to anybody — I could sit by myself, no noise, no people, no stimulation...

And just feel **peace**.

That kind of solitude? That's not loneliness.

That's **recovery**.

* * *

So What Does Connection Really Mean?

It's not noise.

It's not constant company.

It's not even love — not the way people throw that word around.

It's being seen.

It's feeling like someone understands your weirdness, your wounds, your rhythm — and still wants to sit beside you anyway.

That's what breaks loneliness.

That's what heals.

Not crowds. Not partners. Not attention.

Understanding.

Chapter 10
The Ones Who Stayed, The Ones Who Didn't

Loneliness will introduce you to some people.

Pain will introduce you to others.

But the real ones?

They show up **after** the noise.

After the storm, the breakdown, the jail time, the lies, the lost years...

That's when you see who's still standing.

And who's long gone.

* * *

I Don't Blame Most of Them

Honestly, I don't.

Some people aren't built to walk through fire with you.

Some people are just there for the good chapters — the *before*.

The version of you they liked better. The version that was easier to explain.

I get it.

I didn't even like me at the time — how could I expect someone else to?

But man...

When you're down bad and your phone doesn't ring,

when you finally get a letter and it's from a bill collector —

that's when you understand just how small your circle really is.

* * *

But Then There Are the Ones Who Surprised Me

They weren't loud.

They didn't send gifts or show up with big speeches.

They just stayed.

A visit when it was allowed.

A letter with no judgment.

A few words scribbled in the corner of a page:

"You're not forgotten."

That's it.

That's everything.

* * *

I Think About Luna

Not every day, but often enough.

She wasn't trying to rescue me. She wasn't waiting for a fairytale.

She just cared.

Drove my car from El Paso to LA. Wrote me letters that felt like they came from another world.

Made me feel — if only for a few minutes at a time — like I still had *worth*.

I didn't ask her to do any of that.

She just did.

Those are the people who leave fingerprints on your life, whether they stay forever or not.

* * *

And Then There's Family

Family's a complicated thing.

Some try.

Some fail.

Some walk away quietly.

Some never stop showing up, even if they don't know how to help.

Mine... they did what they could.

My mother always felt everything.

My stepdad didn't say much, but I know he kept showing up —
in the ways he knew how.

Even when I told them not to visit, I could still feel their
prayers like static in the air.

That's real.

* * *

The Ones Who Stayed Changed Me

Not because they fixed me.

But because they reminded me I was still someone worth
checking on.

Someone worth writing to.

Someone worth remembering.

That's the medicine loneliness can't kill.

That's the reason you keep going.

Chapter 11
You Don't just "Get Over" Things

If anyone's ever told you to "move on,"

or to "let it go,"

or to "stop living in the past" —

they've probably never carried real weight.

Because here's the truth:

You don't get over the hard stuff.

You just figure out how to carry it without letting it crush you.

* * *

The Past Doesn't Disappear

It doesn't dissolve once you say sorry.

It doesn't fade just because time has passed.

It's not erased when you fall in love again, or find a job, or start doing better.

It's there.

Sometimes loud.

Sometimes quiet.

But always *there* — like a scar that healed but still itches in the rain.

* * *

I Still Have Dreams

Not every night. But often enough.

Sometimes I'm back in the brig.

Sometimes I'm walking into a courtroom again, unsure if I'll be out before sunset.

Sometimes I'm running — not from the law, but from **my own bad decisions**.

And sometimes, I'm just sitting there, holding the same old guilt I thought I laid down years ago.

You don't wake up from those dreams and stretch into peace.

You wake up with a tight chest and a thousand-yard stare.

But you still get up.

That's the difference now.

* * *

Getting Better Isn't Linear

I thought once I served my time, things would just... click.

That I'd slide back into normal.

That my brain would stop beating me up at night.

That my name wouldn't feel dirty in my own mouth.

But growth isn't like that.

It's not a staircase.

It's a spiral.

You circle back to the same wounds — you just hit them from a new angle.

It still stings, but now you *understand it better*.

That's progress, even if it doesn't feel like healing.

* * *

There's No Clean Finish Line

No moment where you drop your bags, wipe your hands, and say,

"Well, I'm done with that."

That's not how real life works.

You carry it.

But now you carry it **better**.

With more honesty.

Lonely

With less shame.

With more room in your chest for other things, like joy. Or hope. Or connection.

You *grow around* what hurt you.

And that's how you win.

Chapter 12

What No One Tells You About Starting Over

Starting over sounds clean.

Like you get a fresh page.

Like you close a door and open a new one, and suddenly the light comes in.

But it's not clean.

It's not easy.

And it's **not fast**.

Starting over is messy.

It's lonely.

It's exhausting.

But it's also one of the most *honest* things you'll ever do.

* * *

I Didn't Know Where to Begin

When I got out — really out — I didn't have some perfect plan.

There was no job waiting.

No apartment.

No parade.

Just a world that had kept moving while I sat behind walls.

And the scariest part?

I was different.

Not in the ways people could see, maybe.

But inside? Everything had shifted.

I didn't want the same things.

Didn't trust the same people.

Didn't believe the same story about who I was supposed
to be.

You Start With What You Have

For me, it was this:

- I knew how to write.

- I had a past I wasn't proud of, but couldn't pretend didn't
exist.

- And I had a hunger — to feel *alive* again. To *matter* again.

So I did what I could.

Got small jobs.

Stayed quiet.

Watched people.

Learned what not to say.

And tried like hell not to slip back into the version of me that only knew how to survive, not live.

The World Doesn't Always Forgive

There were doors I couldn't open — even after paying the price.

There were people who looked at me and only saw a record.

Only saw what I'd done.

And yeah, that burns.

But I had to learn how to walk past those doors and keep moving.

Not to prove anything.

Not to win anyone back.

Just to keep going.

Because *forward* was the only direction that wasn't death.

There's Power in Building Something Quietly

When nobody's watching...

When nobody's clapping...

When no one thinks you'll make it...

That's when you find out what you're really made of.

I started to rebuild in silence.

No big declarations.

No need to be impressive.

Just one solid step at a time.

Writing.

Thinking.

Trying.

Failing.

Trying again.

And slowly — life started to respond.

Not all at once. But enough.

* * *

Starting Over Doesn't Mean Forgetting

It means **deciding**.

Deciding who you want to be now.

What you want to carry forward.

What you're done letting define you.

I didn't erase my past.

I just stopped **letting it be the whole story**.

Chapter 13
Trust Comes Last

You can rebuild your life.

You can rebuild your habits.

Even your body, your bank account, your schedule, your dreams.

But trust?

That comes last.

* * *

It's the One Thing You Can't Rush

You might think if you just show people the *new* you —

cleaned up, grown up, settled down — they'll believe in you again.

But it doesn't work like that.

They're not watching your words anymore.

They're watching your patterns.

And that hurts, especially when you *know* you've changed.

* * *

I Had to Learn Not to Take It Personal

Easier said than done.

When people kept their distance, I felt like I was still wearing a sign around my neck:

Don't Trust Me. Broken Goods. Past Will Repeat.

But here's what I figured out:

Their hesitation wasn't always about me.

It was about *them*.

Their own pain. Their own baggage.

Maybe their own version of a "George" who *didn't* change.

So I stopped begging for belief.

And I started showing up anyway.

* * *

Some People Came Around

They watched me long enough to see something different.

Not perfect.

Not fixed.

But *honest*.

And honesty builds trust brick by brick. Quietly. Without announcements.

Some people?

They started to lean in again.

* * *

And Some Never Did

They stayed gone.

Stayed skeptical.

Stayed cold.

I used to fight that.

Now I bless it.

Because some people are just a chapter — not the whole book.

And that's okay.

I don't need everyone to come with me into the next part of my life.

I just need the right ones.

The ones who see the full picture —

the past, the progress, the present — and choose to walk with me anyway.

* * *

Most of All, I Had to Learn to Trust Myself

That was the hardest part.

To believe I could make a good decision and stick to it.

To believe I could be trusted with someone's heart again.

With a future.

With *my own peace*.

That took time.

But it came.

And once I started to trust myself —

The whole world started to feel different.

Chapter 14
The Quiet Power of Forgiveness

People think forgiveness is loud.

That it's this dramatic moment — tears, hugs, music swelling in the background like some movie ending.

But most of the time?

Forgiveness is quiet.

No cameras. No audience. No big announcement.

Just a moment between you and the truth.

I Had to Forgive a Lot of People

The guard who locked me in that solitary cell.

The judge who didn't look me in the eye.

The friend who disappeared the second things got hard.

People who said they loved me — until they didn't.

People who owed me nothing but still found a way to hurt me anyway.

And you know what?

Forgiving them didn't mean what they did was okay.

It just meant I stopped carrying *their weight* on top of mine.

But the Hardest One Was Me

I could explain away other people's mistakes.

I could justify why they walked or why they failed me.

But me?

I knew better.

I knew what I did.

I knew when I could've stopped and didn't.

I knew when I lied, ran, blamed, and escaped.

That's what made it so hard.

Shame Is Heavy

It'll follow you into a job interview.

Into a new relationship.

Into bed at night when the world's quiet and you think maybe
— *just maybe* — you're finally safe.

But then it whispers,

"Yeah, but remember what you did?"

And it's back. Just like that.

Forgiveness Took Time

Not just once — but over and over.

Like peeling layers off a story I'd told myself for years.

"I'm a screw-up."

"I ruin everything."

"I don't deserve peace."

Each time I forgave myself, I peeled back a lie.

Until eventually... There was enough of me left to breathe
again.

Here's What I Know Now

Forgiveness isn't about pretending something didn't happen.

It's about *releasing the hold it has on you.*

It's about refusing to be defined by your lowest moment.

About choosing — over and over — to give yourself a shot at a future that feels lighter.

And yeah, it's hard.

But it's holy work.

And every time I choose it,

I get one step closer to being free for real.

Chapter 15

The People Who Saved Me Didn't Know They were Saving Me

They didn't give speeches.

They didn't hold my hand through every breakdown.

They didn't even know how dark it really got for me.

But they showed up.

And that saved me.

* * *

A Letter. A Ride. A Look.

It wasn't some grand act.

It was **Luna**, driving my car 800 miles just so I wouldn't lose one more thing.

It was **Pi**, waiting by the gate when I got out, telling me with a stupid joke that I still mattered.

It was **my mom**, sending ten bucks a month for the canteen even when I told her not to.

It was **Mike**, nodding at me in the yard like I wasn't a lost cause.

Tiny things.

But they landed big.

* * *

The World Made Me Feel Disposable

The system. The silence. The way people looked through me.

That's what loneliness does.

It makes you think maybe you deserve to disappear.

That maybe the world would run smoother without you in it.

But then someone remembers your name.

Sends a letter.

Saves a seat.

And suddenly — even just for a second — you feel *real* again.

* * *

They Didn't Fix Me

That's the part people misunderstand.

Nobody fixed me.

Lonely

Nobody rescued me.

Nobody held the map to get me out of the mess I was in.

But they handed me a reason to keep walking.

And sometimes that's all a person needs.

* * *

You Never Know When You're That Person for Someone Else

You don't have to be perfect.

You don't have to have the right words.

You just have to show up.

Because that moment you think meant nothing?

It might be the exact moment someone decided not to give up.

* * *

That's why I write this.

Not to be admired.

Not to be excused.

Not to be impressive.

But to hand back what was handed to me.

A sign.

A nod.

A reason.

To stay.

Chapter 16

You Can Miss a
Place That Hurt You

This one surprised me.

I thought once I got out — out of the brig, out of the cell, out of the youth authority — I'd never look back.

But I did.

Not because I wanted to go back.

Not because I forgot what it did to me.

But because somehow, **that place held pieces of me** I hadn't found anywhere else.

* * *

It's Not About Missing the Pain

I don't miss the cold floors.

The guards yelling.

The nights I thought about ending it all.

But I miss the parts of me that *rose* in that pain.

The grit.

The rawness.

The way I learned what I could take — and what I couldn't.

You don't learn that on easy streets.

* * *

I Miss the Brotherhood

Some of the worst days of my life were surrounded by some of the **realest people** I ever met.

People who didn't sugarcoat it.

Who didn't pretend they were better than me.

Who laughed loud and fought hard and cried without shame.

Pi.

Mike.

Even the ones I didn't talk to much — we shared something you can't fake.

We were cracked open.

And somehow, that made us *honest*.

* * *

Sometimes I Miss the Simplicity

You wake up.

Lonely

You eat what they give you.

You do your time.

And yeah — it's awful.

But it's also **clear**.

Out here, everything's layered.

Everyone's performing.

You can lose yourself chasing things that don't matter.

In there, it was just: survive.

And somehow, that kind of focus felt... pure.

* * *

But What I Really Miss Is Who I Was Becoming

Because in those walls —

writing in the Bible,

learning to type,

choosing to fight *less*,

talking to ghosts in my head and calling it growth...

That's where I started to become **this version of me**.

Not proud.

Not perfect.

But *awake*.

And I wouldn't trade that for anything.

Chapter 17
Loneliness Doesn't
End When You Get Out

You'd think once the door opened and I walked free, the loneliness would fade.

But no.

Sometimes it got louder.

Because now I wasn't just *alone in a cell* —

I was alone in a world that had moved on without me.

* * *

No One Tells You How Quiet It Is

You step outside and think there'll be noise.

Cars. People. Life.

And sure, it's all there. But it doesn't **include you**.

You're watching from the curb.

Lonely

Like a stranger in your own city.

Like you've come back from the dead and nobody noticed.

* * *

You Don't Belong to Anything Yet

In prison, you belong — even if you don't want to.

You have a bunk. A number. A routine.

You know where to be and what happens if you don't show up.

But out here?

It's up to you.

And that kind of freedom?

It's terrifying.

* * *

Some Days I Missed the Schedule

I missed knowing what came next.

I missed hearing my name at mail call.

I missed *anyone* expecting me to show up.

And that scared the hell out of me —

That I could miss prison *for the structure* it gave me.

But that's how loneliness tricks you.

It makes you nostalgic for the wrong things —

because at least they were **something**.

* * *

What Saved Me Was Purpose

Even when I didn't know what the future looked like,

I knew I had to make *this time* mean something.

I had to write.

To tell it like it was.

To stop hiding behind excuses and just... *put it out there.*

The pages didn't judge me.

They didn't expect me to smile.

They let me be lonely — without shame.

And in that space?

I started to heal.

Chapter 18
You Don't Just Rebuild - You Reinvent

People say "rebuild your life" like it's construction work.

Like you just go back to who you were before the collapse.

But what if there's no blueprint?

What if the "before" version of you wasn't working either?

You don't just rebuild.

You reinvent.

* * *

I Had to Ask Myself Some Hard Questions

Who am I *without* the uniform?

Without the jail number?

Without the shame?

What do I actually believe?

What do I stand for when no one's watching?

What kind of man do I even want to be?

The answers didn't come all at once.

But I kept asking.

And I let the answers surprise me.

* * *

Reinvention Starts Small

I didn't wake up one day suddenly healed.

I just did the next right thing.

Wrote a letter.

Kept a promise.

Didn't punch the guy who mouthed off.

And that counted.

That *stacked up*.

It's like lifting weights you don't think you can handle —

until one day, you're doing reps without even thinking about it.

* * *

I Had to Let Go of the Old Story

The one where I screw everything up.

The one where I always leave.

Lonely

The one where people get hurt just by knowing me.

That story served its purpose.

It kept me from pretending.

But it didn't have to be the **whole** story.

So I started writing a new one.

Right here.

In real time.

* * *

You're Allowed to Change

That's what I'd tell anyone reading this who feels stuck in who they've been.

You are allowed to change.

Not because someone gives you permission.

But because you *decide* the past doesn't get the final word.

Reinvention isn't fake.

It's freedom.

And I'm walking proof of it.

Chapter 19
Even the Strong Break

People used to say I was strong.

I could handle anything.

Bounce back from everything.

Make jokes in hell.

But what they didn't see —

what *nobody* sees until it's too late —

is that even the strong break.

* * *

I Broke Quietly

Not with a scream.

Not with fists through walls.

I broke in silence.

Lonely

In empty rooms.

In the way I'd stare at a letter too long.

In the way I'd pretend the past didn't still sting.

And I'd say I was fine.

Because that's what the "strong" do, right?

We're fine.

We're always fine.

Until we're not.

* * *

Loneliness Doesn't Care About Muscle

It doesn't care how many fights you've won.

How many jokes you crack.

How many nights you've survived.

It finds the cracks.

Slips in through the smallest holes.

And settles.

Like it owns you.

* * *

What Helped Me Was Honesty

Not with everyone.

Not all the time.

Just with *myself*.

I started saying it:

"I'm not okay."

I said it on paper first.

Then in my head.

Then, maybe once or twice, out loud.

And it didn't make me weak.

It made me real.

* * *

Everyone Breaks

That doesn't make you broken.

It makes you **human**.

The trick isn't to avoid the break.

The trick is to learn how to come back — not the same as before,

but **stronger in the right places**.

The ones that matter.

Chapter 20
There's No Finish Line

Like, if you just get through the sentence, get through the heartbreak, get through the mess you made...

Then boom — you'll be done.

Healed.

Whole.

Happy.

But there's no finish line.

* * *

Life Keeps Showing Up

Even when you think you've figured it all out — even when you've patched your wounds and found your rhythm — life still throws punches.

New ones.

Old ones in new disguises.

Triggers you thought you buried.

And you know what?

That's not failure.

That's just being alive.

* * *

Growth Isn't a Straight Line

Some days I handled things like a man with peace in his pocket.

Other days I wanted to run. To disappear. To throw fists at the sky.

Some days I showed up with wisdom.

Other days I was just surviving.

That's not weakness.

That's **progress**, even when it's messy.

* * *

The Only Thing That Changed Is Me

I stopped chasing perfect.

Stopped needing to prove I was better than my past.

I started showing up — *as I am, where I am*.

With love when I had it.

With patience when I could.

With honesty when I didn't have anything else.

And that became enough.

You Don't Graduate from This Work

There's no diploma for becoming a better man.

No trophy for surviving the worst parts of yourself.

But there's peace.

There's sleep.

There's a kind of strength that's not loud, but *real*.

And if I've learned anything...

It's that I'll be doing this work the rest of my life.

And that's okay.

Chapter 21

I Didn't Need to Be Saved - I Needed to Be Seen

People tried to fix me.

Teachers. Cops. Judges.

Friends. Lovers. Therapists.

Even strangers.

They threw solutions at me like I was a problem to be solved.

But I wasn't looking for a fix.

I just wanted someone to *see* me.

* * *

To Be Seen Is Different Than Being Watched

I was *watched* all the time.

In the brig.

In jail.

By guards. By cops. By anyone waiting for me to screw up again.

But being watched and being seen?

Two different things.

Being watched feels like surveillance.

Being seen feels like someone says,

"You're still in there. I see you."

I Didn't Even Know I Needed That

I didn't grow up with words like "validation" or "emotional support."

I knew loyalty. Respect. Power.

Not softness. Not presence.

So when someone sat with me without judgment,

or listened without a lecture — it *confused me*.

But it also healed me.

You Start to See Yourself the Way Others Do

And if everyone looks at you like a criminal, like a lost cause,

like a ticking bomb — You start to believe them.

But if *one person* sees more?

Sees *possibility*, not just damage?

That's a crack of light.

And sometimes light is all you need.

* * *

That's Why I Try to See People Now

Not fix them.

Not preach at them.

Not tell them what to do.

Just *see* them.

Because that might be the only thing keeping them from giving up.

Chapter 22

Some People Leave - and Still Stay With You

Not everyone walks out the door and disappears.

Some people leave —

and they never really go.

They stay in your head.

Your chest.

Your habits.

Your silence.

They show up in the way you trust.

Or don't.

In what makes you smile — or shut down.

* * *

I Thought I Was Over It

Thought I'd moved on from her.

From him.

From them.

Thought I'd buried it deep enough.

But some memories don't die.

They *camp out*.

They wait.

You think you're safe, and suddenly — a smell, a voice, a laugh —

And you're back in it.

* * *

Love Isn't Always Clean

Sometimes love is unfinished.

You didn't get closure.

Didn't get the apology.

Didn't get to say what you should've said.

And so it lingers.

It *aches*.

And that doesn't mean you're weak.

It means you're human.

* * *

You Can Forgive and Still Feel It

You can forgive someone who hurt you and still think about them.

You can understand why it ended and still miss what it was.

Both things can be true.

And that's okay.

* * *

The Trick Is Not Letting It Define You

You carry them — yes.

But you don't let them *drive*.

You don't build your whole future around a ghost.

You acknowledge the shadow, but you *walk toward the light anyway*.

That's growth.

That's survival.

That's freedom.

Chapter 23
There's Always a Cost to Hiding

For years, I thought hiding was smart.

Don't show too much.

Don't tell too much.

Keep your cards close.

Stay ahead of the pain.

But here's what nobody tells you:

There's always a cost to hiding.

And sometimes, it's *everything*.

* * *

I Hid Behind Jokes

I could make people laugh.

Deflect with humor.

Lonely

Turn pain into punchlines.

People thought I was okay.

They didn't see I was bleeding under the smile.

* * *

I Hid Behind Anger

It's easier to get loud than to get honest.

Easier to throw punches than to say, "I'm scared."

"I'm sad."

"I'm lost."

Anger gave me control — but it also kept everyone out.

And I didn't realize how much I needed someone *in*.

* * *

I Hid Behind Strength

People called me tough, so I made sure to act like it.

Even when I was breaking.

Even when I was empty.

Because if I let the mask slip — what then?

What would they think?

What would I think?

* * *

The Truth Set Me Free — But Not Right Away

Telling the truth didn't fix everything.

It made things *messy* at first.

Uncomfortable. Exposed.

But little by little —

I started to breathe.

I started to feel.

And I realized...

The more I stopped hiding, the more I started healing.

* * *

You Don't Have to Show Everything

But show *something*.

Let someone in.

Let *yourself* in.

Because hiding keeps you safe, but it also keeps you small.

And you weren't meant to live small.

You were meant to live *free*.

Chapter 24

You Can Love People Who Hurt You - And Still Let Them Go

Nobody really tells you how confusing love can be.

They say if someone hurts you, walk away.

They say protect your peace.

They say cut toxic people out.

And sometimes, they're right.

But what they don't say is this:

You can love people who hurt you.

And still let them go.

Love Doesn't Erase the Damage

Just because you care about someone doesn't mean they're good for you.

Just because you *understand* them doesn't mean you should *stay*.

Some people are broken in ways that break you too.

And no amount of love can glue two shattered pieces together into something whole.

* * *

Leaving Doesn't Mean You Didn't Care

It means you finally cared enough about *yourself*

to stop bleeding for someone who kept cutting you.

It means you chose to heal — not to punish them,

but to protect you.

* * *

The Grief is Real

You don't just walk away clean.

You remember the good times.

You ache for the parts that felt safe.

You replay the laughs, the closeness, the "what ifs."

It hurts.

It's supposed to.

But it's also part of the process.

Lonely

* * *

Letting Go Is a Kind of Love Too

It's love that says:

"I wish you well, but I can't lose myself for you."

"I hope you find peace, but I have to go find mine."

"I love you, but I also love *me now*."

And that's a powerful kind of love.

One that saves lives.

Chapter 25

Loneliness Doesn't Always Look Like You Think

It's not always someone sitting alone in the dark.

It's not always tears, or silence, or empty rooms.

Sometimes loneliness wears a smile.

Sometimes it laughs loud.

Sometimes it shows up surrounded by people

who have *no idea* how alone you feel inside.

I've Been the Life of the Party — and Still Felt Invisible

I've told stories.

Cracked jokes.

Held a room in the palm of my hand.

And walked away feeling like no one really *saw* me.

Lonely

That's a special kind of hollow.

When you're surrounded — and still starving for connection.

* * *

Loneliness Isn't About Being Alone

It's about *not being understood.*

Not being felt.

Not being heard.

Not being *gotten.*

You can be married and feel it.

You can have friends and feel it.

You can be in a crowded room and still feel like you're screaming underwater.

* * *

We Hide It Well

Because loneliness has shame baked into it.

Like if you're lonely, you must be broken.

Unlovable.

Weak.

So we cover it.

But loneliness thrives in silence.

* * *

Naming It Gives It Less Power

When I started saying the word out loud — just to myself at first —

It started to loosen its grip.

Because when we name it, we're not hiding anymore.

We're healing.

We're reaching.

We're *human*.

Chapter 26

Sometimes It Was My Fault - And I Needed to Say That

It's easy to point fingers.

To say, *"They did this to me."*

And sometimes — that's the truth.

But other times?

It was me.

My choices.

My ego.

My fear.

My silence.

* * *

I Hurt People Too

Not because I was evil.

Not because I meant to.

But because I was scared.

Because I didn't know better.

Because I was trying to protect something broken in me.

And sometimes I didn't even realize I'd caused damage

until years later.

Accountability Isn't Shame — It's Freedom

When I started owning my part, I didn't shrink.

I grew.

I didn't fall apart.

I found myself.

Because taking responsibility isn't about beating yourself up
—

it's about *lifting yourself up* by finally getting honest.

"I'm Sorry" Isn't Always About Getting Forgiveness

Sometimes the apology isn't for them to hear — it's for *you* to say.

It's how you make peace with who you were so you can become who you're meant to be.

Lonely

* * *

I Still Get It Wrong Sometimes

I still react when I should listen.

Still disappear when I should speak.

Still hold walls up when I should let love in.

But I see it now.

And that's the difference.

Awareness is the beginning of change.

Chapter 27
You Can Start Over More Than Once

They make it sound like you get one shot.

One big chance.

One clean slate.

One fresh start.

But life doesn't work like that.

You can start over again — and again — and again.

And every time,

you're not back at zero.

You're back at *wiser*.

* * *

I've Lost Count of My Restarts

After the Navy.

After jail.

After heartbreak.

After failure.

After fucking up something good.

Every time, I thought:

This must be the end.

But it wasn't.

It was just a different kind of beginning.

* * *

The World Keeps Moving — So Can You

Even when it feels like time stopped.

Even when you feel stuck.

Even when shame tells you.

You've used up all your chances — You haven't.

You're still breathing.

That means *you're not done.*

* * *

Starting Over Isn't Weak — It's Brave

It means you were willing to let go.

To say,

"That wasn't working. I'll try again."

It means you're not letting failure be the final word.

It means you believe there's still something worth building.

* * *

Wherever You Are — It's Not Too Late

Start over today.

Start over tomorrow.

Start over as many damn times as you need to.

There is no shame in the reset.

There's only power in the choice to *begin again*.

Chapter 28

The Hardest Goodbyes Are the Ones Without Closure

Some people leave quietly.

No explanation.

No warning.

No goodbye.

And you're left holding a mess of memories, questions, and a silence so loud it echoes in your bones.

I've Replayed Conversations That Never Happened

What I should've said.

What I wish they'd said.

What I needed to hear and never did.

It's like trying to end a song that never got its last note.

And it haunts you.

* * *

Closure Isn't Always Something You Get — Sometimes It's Something You Create

I had to learn that.

Because waiting on someone else to bring peace to your story

can keep you stuck forever.

Sometimes you have to say:

"This hurt.

I don't understand it.

But I'm letting it go anyway."

* * *

You Can Mourn What You Never Got

The apology.

The explanation.

The proper goodbye.

You can grieve that.

It doesn't make you dramatic.

It makes you real.

And grief is proof that something mattered.

Lonely

* * *

Healing Doesn't Always Need an Answer

Sometimes all you need is to let yourself feel the weight of it
—

and *keep walking* anyway.

You may never understand why they left.

But you get to choose what you carry forward.

And sometimes,

choosing peace is the best goodbye you'll ever give.

Chapter 29

Healing Doesn't Mean You Don't Still Feel It

People think healing means you're over it.

That it doesn't sting anymore.

That you've moved on, and the pain is all packed away neatly.

But healing isn't a straight line.

And it's not the same as forgetting.

I've Healed — and Still Hurts Sometimes

A song plays.

A place I drive past.

A random date on the calendar.

And suddenly, I'm *there* again.

Lonely

Not drowning in it — but feeling it in my chest, like a bruise that's still tender even though it's not bleeding anymore.

* * *

Healing Just Means You've Made Peace With the Wound

It means you can live with it without letting it define you.

It means you've stopped picking the scab every day just to prove you're still hurt.

It means you *accept* what happened, even if you'll never love that it did.

* * *

You're Allowed to Still Feel It

Even after time passes.

Even after growth.

Even after joy returns.

That doesn't mean you're broken.

It means you're honest.

It means you're *human*.

* * *

The Goal Isn't Perfection — It's Wholeness

You're not trying to erase the past.

You're learning to live beside it.

To hold joy and sadness in the same hands and still keep moving forward.

Because healing isn't about pretending.

It's about becoming *realer* than you've ever been.

Chapter 30

Forgiveness Isn't Always About Them

"You've gotta forgive."

"Let it go."

"Don't carry that weight."

And sure — it sounds right.

But when someone's cut you deep, forgiveness feels like handing them a free pass.

And that's not what it is.

Forgiveness Doesn't Mean You're Saying It Was Okay

It doesn't excuse it.

It doesn't erase it.

It doesn't mean you invite them back into your life.

It just means you're done letting it poison you.

Done reliving it.

Done rehearsing the pain.

Done carrying what wasn't yours to hold forever.

* * *

I Thought Holding a Grudge Gave Me Power

Like if I stayed mad, I stayed in control.

But the truth?

That anger didn't protect me.

It imprisoned me.

And the person who hurt me?

They weren't feeling it — *I was.*

* * *

Forgiveness Set Me Free

I didn't always say it out loud.

I didn't always tell them.

But I wrote it.

I prayed it.

I whispered it when I was alone:

"I forgive you.

Not because you earned it —

but because I deserve peace."

* * *

You Don't Have to Forgive All at Once

It's not a light switch.

Some wounds take time.

Some take distance.

Some take years.

That's okay.

Just remember:

Forgiveness isn't about weakness.

It's about choosing *freedom* —

over and over again.

Chapter 31

You Can Be Proud of Yourself - Quietly

You don't have to make a speech.

You don't have to post about it.

You don't need applause.

You can look in the mirror and nod at the person you're becoming.

That's enough.

* * *

I've Survived Things Nobody Knows

Not because I kept it all inside, but because some things are sacred.

Some strength doesn't need to be broadcast.

There are victories that don't show up in photos.

There's growth that happens in the dark.

Lonely

* * *

Quiet Pride is Still Powerful

It's in the way you breathe easier now.

In the way you don't react the way you used to.

In the way you *know better* and *do better*, even if no one sees it but you.

That's real pride.

That's the kind that lasts.

* * *

Not Everything Needs to Be Proved

Some people won't understand what you've overcome.

That's okay.

Some people will never know how hard you fought to stay soft.

To stay kind.

To stay *you*.

But you know.

And that's enough.

* * *

Be Proud — Even If You're Not Done Yet

You're still healing.

Still building.

Still learning.

But damn — you've come far.

Let that quiet pride rise.

It belongs to *you*.

Chapter 32

Sometimes, You're the Only One Who'll Understand

Not every story you carry

can be told.

Not every feeling can be translated.

And sometimes, the people you hope will get it —

won't.

I've Tried to Explain and Still Felt Alone

I've sat across from people and spilled pieces of my past, only to watch confusion settle in their eyes.

Not judgment.

Just a wall.

They didn't *get it*.

Not really.

And that's a different kind of lonely.

* * *

But That Doesn't Mean Your Story Doesn't Matter

Just because someone else can't hold it doesn't mean you shouldn't say it.

Or write it.

Or face it.

You're not crazy.

You're not too much.

You're just carrying a story with *weight*.

* * *

Some Chapters Are Just for You

And maybe one day, someone will read between the lines

and say, "Me too."

But even if they don't — your truth is still truth.

And it still deserves space.

* * *

Don't Wait for Others to Validate What You Know in Your Bones

Lonely

Some roads are walked alone.

Some healing is witnessed by no one.

But that doesn't make it less real.

You're allowed to understand yourself even if no one else can.

Chapter 33

There's No Timeline for Getting Your Life Together

Some people get it "right" at 25.

Some don't figure it out until they're 55.

And some of us?

We fall apart and start over more times than we can count.

That's not failure.

That's *life*.

* * *

I've Watched Others Pass Me by

Careers.

Families.

Nice houses.

Clean records.

And I've thought,

"I'm too far behind."

"I missed my window."

But life doesn't run on one clock.

There are *millions* of clocks.

And yours is yours.

Progress Isn't Always Linear — or Loud

Sometimes, getting your life together looks like finally getting out of bed.

Or choosing not to call someone toxic.

Or making a doctor's appointment.

Or applying for a job you're scared of.

Small steps are still steps.

And slow progress is still *progress.*

You're Not Late — You're Just On Your Own Path

Some of us had detours.

Some of us had to heal before we could build.

Some of us had to survive things others couldn't even imagine.

You're not broken.

You're not behind.

You're *becoming*.

* * *

Keep Going — There's Still Time

You don't have to have it all figured out.

You don't need a five-year plan.

You just need to take the next right step — and then the next.

One day, you'll look back and realize:

You built something beautiful.

Just not on anyone else's timeline.

Chapter 34

Some People Will Never See Who You Really Are - Love Yourself Anyway

You can pour your heart out.

Show up.

Do the work.

Tell the truth.

Give everything.

And still — some people won't see you.

Not the *real* you.

I've Been Misjudged By People Who Never Took the Time

They saw a version of me that fit their story — not mine.

They believed what they wanted.

They filled in blanks I never gave them.

And no matter what I said or did, it didn't change a thing.

* * *

That Hurts — But It Doesn't Define You

You can't force someone to see your heart if they've already decided not to.

That's not your failure.

That's their limitation.

Let them carry their version.

You carry the truth.

* * *

Don't Lose Yourself Trying to Win Them Over

You don't need to shrink

to be acceptable.

You don't need to prove your worth

to people who've already made up their mind.

Stand tall in who you are.

Especially when it's hard.

* * *

Love Yourself Loud Enough to Drown Out the Noise

Because one day.

Lonely

Someone will see you clearly —

And they'll wonder

how anyone could have missed you.

But even if they don't?

You know who you are.

And that's more than enough.

Chapter 35

You don't Owe Anyone the Unhealed Version of You

You've done the work.

You've bled for your growth.

You've cried, broken, rebuilt,

and kept showing up.

So no —

you don't owe anyone the version of you

who didn't know better.

* * *

I've Outgrown Some People — And That's Okay

People who knew me

when I didn't know myself.

When I was angry.

Or afraid.

Or still stuck in survival mode.

They remember a different version of me.

But that's not who I am anymore.

* * *

Growth Can Be Lonely

Because not everyone grows with you.

Some stay in the past.

Some only see who you *used* to be.

But that doesn't mean you go back

just to keep the peace.

* * *

You Don't Have to Reopen Wounds to Prove You've Healed

You don't have to explain

why you've changed.

You don't have to revisit old pain

to make someone else comfortable.

You can say:

"That's not me anymore."

And leave it at that.

* * *

Protect the Person You've Fought to Become

It's okay to set boundaries.

To say no.

To keep your peace sacred.

You've come too far

to hand your progress

back to people who never understood the price.

* * *

You've earned this healing.

Don't apologize for it.

Chapter 36

Not Everything Has to Be Turned Into a Lesson

Some pain just *hurts*.

Some losses don't have a silver lining.

Some moments don't need to be "for growth."

They just are.

And they suck.

And it's okay to say that.

I've Spent Years Trying to Find Meaning in Everything

As if the heartbreak had to teach me something.

As if the loss needed to make me wiser.

As if the suffering wasn't valid

unless I turned it into wisdom.

But you know what?

Some things just broke me.

And that's the whole story.

* * *

It's Okay to Let Some Moments Just Be What They Were

Not everything needs a purpose.

Not every wound needs to be poetic.

Not every scar tells a story worth retelling.

Some things just happen.

And they don't make sense.

And they never will.

* * *

Give Yourself Permission to Stop Digging

You don't need to analyze it again.

Or spin it into inspiration.

Or wrap it in some deep metaphor.

You're allowed to say:

"That hurt like hell —

and I'm just trying to live through it."

And that's enough.

Lonely

* * *

You're Still Growing — Even When There's No Lesson

Survival is growth.

Rest is growth.

Making it through the day

without falling apart is growth.

You don't need a lesson to prove you're healing.

You just need *truth*.

And the courage to live with it.

Chapter 37

Sometimes, You Just Need to Be Heard - Not Fixed

When you're in pain,

people rush to solve it.

"Have you tried this?"

"Look on the bright side."

"You just need to stay positive."

But sometimes,

you don't need a solution.

You just need someone to *listen*.

I've Been Talked Over by People Who Meant Well

They didn't mean harm.

But their comfort with *my* pain

was more important than sitting with it.

And so they rushed in —

with advice, with cliches,

with stories about themselves.

And I was left holding my truth

alone.

* * *

Being Heard Is a Kind of Healing

It's when someone says:

"I believe you."

"That sounds hard."

"I'm here."

No fixing.

No redirecting.

No shrinking it down to something easier.

Just presence.

That's what changes things.

* * *

You Deserve to Take Up Space — Even With Your Mess

You don't have to have the right words.

You don't have to end every sentence with,

"But I'll be okay."

You can speak your truth

and let it land without a bow on top.

You're not a burden.

You're *a human being.*

Find the People Who Can Hold Your Silence

And if you don't have them yet,

be that person for yourself.

Write it.

Say it out loud.

Let your voice rise — even if no one's there yet.

You're not too much.

You never were.

Chapter 38
Healing Doesn't Always Feel Like Healing

Sometimes healing looks like crying more.

Sleeping more.

Getting angry.

Feeling things you buried a long time ago.

It's not always calm.

It's not always peaceful.

It doesn't always *look better* right away.

I Thought I Was Getting Worse

There were days I felt like I was breaking all over again.

Like everything, I tried to move past

was hunting me down.

But I wasn't going backward.

I was finally feeling what I hadn't been able to feel before.

That's healing, too.

* * *

You Don't Have to Hold It All Together to Be Making Progress

Healing is messy.

It's nonlinear.

One day you're breathing easy,

the next you can't get out of bed.

That doesn't mean you're failing.

It means you're *in it*.

* * *

The Storm Is Part of the Process

You can't clean a wound

without touching it.

You can't heal from silence

without finding your voice.

So if it hurts?

If it's raw?

If everything feels too loud?

That's not wrong.

That's the work.

* * *

You're Closer Than You Think

Even in the chaos.

Even in the grief.

Even when you don't recognize yourself.

You're not starting over.

You're *shedding*.

Let the storm pass.

You're becoming whole.

Chapter 39

The Strongest People Aren't Always Loud About It

Some strength isn't in the spotlight.

It doesn't shout.

It doesn't flex.

It's quiet.

It's steady.

It's *survival*.

* * *

I've Met Strength That Whispers

The kind that wakes up and keeps going —

even when it would be easier to give up.

The kind that shows up

for people who'll never say thank you.

Lonely

The kind that cries in private,

but still makes the call,

still cooks the dinner,

still tries again.

You Don't Need to Perform Your Strength

You don't have to be the loudest voice in the room.

You don't have to always "look okay."

You can be soft *and* strong.

You can break *and* rebuild.

You can rest *and* still be brave.

* * *

If No One Told You Today — I See It

I see how hard you've been trying.

I see the weight you carry.

I see the courage it takes

to just keep showing up.

And I want you to know:

That counts.

Even if no one claps.

Even if no one sees it but you.

* * *

Strength Isn't What You Show — It's What You Survive

And you?

You've survived *a lot*.

That's strength.

That's power.

That's yours.

Chapter 40
You Can Be Grateful and Still Want More

You can say "thank you"

for what you have

and still admit that your heart aches

for something different.

Gratitude doesn't mean settling.

It doesn't mean silencing the hunger inside you.

I've Guilt-Tripped Myself Into Staying Small

Told myself I should be content.

That other people had it worse.

That I was lucky just to be here.

And I *am* lucky.

But I'm also allowed to grow.

To reach.

To want.

* * *

Your Desire Doesn't Cancel Out Your Gratitude

You can love your life

and still dream of something more.

You can respect your past

and still outgrow it.

You can say,

"This is good —

and I know there's more for me."

And that's not selfish.

That's *honest.*

* * *

Don't Let "It Could Be Worse" Become a Cage

Yes, things could be worse.

But they could also be better.

You don't need to suffer

to prove you're thankful.

You're allowed to change.

To rise.

To reach for what calls to you.

* * *

Gratitude and Growth Can Coexist

So keep saying thank you.

And keep moving forward.

You don't have to choose

between appreciation

and ambition.

You can hold both — and still have room for more.

Chapter 41

You Can Walk Away Without Getting the Apology

Sometimes closure doesn't come in a sentence.

Sometimes "I'm sorry" never arrives.

Sometimes the people who hurt you

keep telling themselves they didn't.

And still —

you're allowed to move on.

I Waited for Words That Never Came

I thought maybe if they understood,

they'd make it right.

Maybe if they saw what it cost me,

they'd feel something.

But they never did.

And I kept waiting

in a room they'd already left.

*   *   *

You Don't Need Their Guilt to Heal

You don't need them to feel bad

for you to feel better.

You don't need a confession

to begin again.

You don't need their permission

to let go of what they'll never take responsibility for.

*   *   *

Closure Isn't a Conversation — It's a Decision

You can write your own ending.

You can say:

"I deserved better."

"I didn't imagine it."

"That was real, and it hurt."

"But I'm not carrying it anymore."

You can give yourself

what they never gave you.

* * *

Don't Let Silence Keep You Stuck

You're not weak for walking away.

You're not bitter for remembering.

You're not broken for wanting peace.

You're *healing*.

And sometimes,

healing means closing a door

without waiting for someone else to knock.

About the Author

George Hatcher's life is a testament to second chances. With a formal education that ended in the ninth grade, he has navigated a life of extreme highs and devastating lows, learning his most profound lessons not in a classroom, but through trial and error.

The first half of his life was a whirlwind of entrepreneurial ventures—some successful, others leading to catastrophic failures and, ultimately, prison. Through it all, the one constant, the anchor in every storm, has been his wife, Molly. Their 60-year marriage is the bedrock upon which the second half of his life—one of stability, peace, and prolific writing— was built.

As a passionate storyteller with over two dozen books to his name, George writes from a place of hard-won experience. He explores themes of love, loss, failure, and forgiveness, not as a theorist, but as a man who has lived them. He believes his greatest mistakes have been his most profound teachers and shares his story with unflinching honesty.

He currently resides in Rancho Mirage, California, with Molly, their three cats, and a macaw named Peaches. Now devoted entirely to his craft, George invites readers to join him on a remarkable journey that proves beauty isn't found in perfection, but in the strength it takes to repair what is broken.

A longer bio is available on his website: http://georgehatcher. com/bio/bio.html